AN UNSPECIFIC DOG

Fig. 1. Hieronymus Bosch, *Ship of Fools* (1490–1500)

First published in 2017 by dead letter office, BABEL Working Group
an imprint of punctum books, Earth, Milky Way.
https://punctumbooks.com

The BABEL Working Group is a collective and desiring-assemblage of scholar–
gypsies with no leaders or followers, no top and no bottom, and only a middle.
BABEL roams and stalks the ruins of the post-historical university as a multiplic-
ity, a pack, looking for other roaming packs with which to cohabit and build
temporary shelters for intellectual vagabonds. We also take in strays.

ISBN-13: 978-0-9985318-1-6
ISBN-10: 0-9985318-1-2
Library of Congress Cataloging Data is available from the Library of Congress

Book design: Vincent W.J. van Gerven Oei

Joshua Rothes

An Unspecific Dog
Artifacts of This Late Stage in History

For Bernhard

PREFACE

I, the traveling brute, the terrible insouciant, grant that liberties have been taken in constructing this crude batch of parables and fables. Institutions have been cited where necessary. Place names and the proper names of persons have been sanitized. An inertial meaning may congeal, but I doubt it. Do not read more than is necessary into contiguity; it does not suit you, not now. There are times when our human desire to identify is better stifled, and in the incidents that follow, that have occurred or not, I have been well served by a command of the circumstances, and this has allowed me a measured dispassion. Before the fragments are subsequently narrativized, films cast and all trace of authorial presence removed, know that in all walks, stories seep into the cracks of logic in order to cement, not to subvert, that reason as a medium for encountering the world is fated to fail in ways that are at once terrible and hilarious and make up the stuff of human experience, in fact the whole of what may be called the human condition. Perfection in action is physics; perfection in language is mathematics. Short of that, we have theater. Again, liberties have been taken; in fact, none were spared.

— JR

"Interesting philosophy is rarely an examination of the pros and cons of a thesis. Usually it is, implicitly or explicitly, a contest between an entrenched vocabulary which has become a nuisance and a half-formed new vocabulary which vaguely promises great things."

— Richard Rorty

1

A successful translator sued a plagiarist for the uncanny similarity of some five lines in the latter's recent edition of the complete poems of Rimbaud, the previous addition of which having earned the translator much of his reputation and present livelihood. The translator resented not only the plagiarism, he said before the court, but the velocity at which the plagiarist had rushed out his edition, a mere four years after his own, which was against all protocol in the industry. Even the titles — *Rimbaud: The Complete Works* and *The Complete Poems of Rimbaud* — were unnervingly similar. The plagiarist argued that the five lines in question were comparably short, inconsequential lines, which had been translated much the same over the years, possessing no ambiguous terms and having not the slightest capacity for artistic interpretation, citing even older additions in which the lines were also identical. Further, during the presentation of expert analysis, the translator had been found to have lifted several lines, lines brimming with intimation and difficult pronouns, from an earlier edition by Fowlie, lines that were approached altogether differently by the plagiarist. The judge swiftly dismissed the charges after remarking on the special breed of hypocrite that the translator exemplified, and his edition was pulled from shelves shortly thereafter. But, being the nature of human memory, it is the other man who is still known as *the plagiarist*.

2

A man from Cedar Park in Texas sent a form letter to nearly three thousand companies asking for printed copies of every set of terms and conditions to which he had ever agreed, either directly or by the implied consent of his continuance, and found that he had no secrets.

3

There is, it seems, an implicit guilt in living past the point at which, in earlier times, you would have died, owing to genetic deficiencies. A Stanford study.

4

A writer, having previously failed to win an expensive-to-main-tain lawsuit against a cloud storage company for allegedly hav-ing read his novel-in-progress on the grounds that he could not prove they had done so and, furthermore, could not produce so much as a manuscript page of the work in question for the court's examination upon request, was awarded full damages after succeeding in taking the case to trial in a more favorable jurisdiction overseas, in which the burden of proof effectively changed sides and the cloud storage company was asked to cat-egorically prove that they had not read the novel in question.

5

It has been estimated that, because of their importance to certain branches of developmental psychology, one in two sets of twins has been clandestinely observed against their knowledge during the course of their lives.

6

The sister of a close friend, a microbiologist on the forefront of cataloguing the vast biome of bacteria that inhabit our bodies and affect the regulation of our systems and the expression of our genes in ways that are not yet even superficially understood, spent a good portion of dinner lecturing all of us on the dangers of a market that we had, each one of us, allowed to become the dominant form of epistemology, referring to the presence of a container of probiotic yogurt in the host's refrigerator. She also pointed out to us that the fish had been undercooked, given all we now know, and no one ate or said much after that.

7

It had been an unfortunate setback when a prominent skeptic suffered a fusiform aneurysm while attempting, as a rather public stunt, to overdose on a homeopathic remedy for migraine headaches. While the autopsy and a subsequent fluid analysis proved beyond a reasonable doubt that the aneurysm had been a freak occurrence, not one of the skeptic's colleagues has been willing to complete the challenge.

8

Moral philosophy, which we are told has now become the exclusive realm of the cognitive sciences, has yet to fully account for how Smith knew so much of the contents of Jones's pockets.

9

It has been conclusively shown that confronting a user with graphs and spreadsheets detailing either the cumulative minutes or the fractional percentage of their time spent playing a simple game has virtually no effect on their willingness to play the game again in the future. Furthermore, the design of the study was later found to be unethical.

10

In Palo Alto, a couple was murdered by their own fertility spe-cialist, a known eccentric, who was apprehended just a few blocks away, leering into the window of a home belonging to another set of clients. As part of his opening statement, which did much to persuade the judge of his mental ailments, among them a pathological misanthropism, he asked the jury just when it was that parents had decided that children were *theirs*. Most troubling, there had been no jury present.

11

An entire apartment building had evacuated themselves before firefighters arrived to discover that there had been no fire in the first place, even though no fewer than ten distinct calls had been placed to emergency services indicating, with no uncertainty, that there was a fire. When interviewed later as to why they had called emergency services and evacuated the building when there had been no fire, most answered, after some thought, that they had simply assumed there had been a fire.

12

A specific form of melancholy, described as stemming from the latent fear that a great project will not be completed before death, is particularly prevalent among Marxists. A Cambridge study.

13

There have always been perceived terror threats against the museum, no doubt owing to its esteemed location and confrontational architecture, spires being thought of as they are. Over the years, in fact, public fear has risen in the public mind right alongside attendance, and more security has been hired, despite having very little to report on, let alone thwart. (It is said that even the children behave well at the museum). Last May, when a vagrant was detained for urinating on the eastern wall of the building, the local newspaper editor chose to run with the headline, *Terror strikes museum.*

14

At CalTech, a physicist, who had been working on an alternative hypothesis to space-time involving a discreet tensor network, had been committed to a private psychiatric facility after admitting, having been pressed with conclusive evidence, including recent Internet searches, that he had planned to take his own life. He doubted, he would later confess, that he would be able to prove his theory in his lifetime, and had convinced himself that, given another decade or two in the progress of mind–machine interfaces, the disparate facets of his theory could be pulled from his brain at a later time and assembled in a most satisfactory arrangement that would earn him much esteem. He felt obliged, he said, to give them his brain in its prime, when he was certain that he was so near a breakthrough.

15

The vast improvements in emergency care coupled with in-creased public awareness of the symptoms and warning signs of a number of serious maladies are not, a physician once re-marked to me at a party, sufficient to explain why one hears to-day of significantly fewer people than earlier times who simply *drop dead,* implying some hypothesis.

16

Recently, the most famous poet our country had produced, who had also happened to be the current poet laureate, passed away while on vacation in Venice. It had been a pity, we all decided. Though I had to say that I had been only passingly familiar with her work, she had represented us well as our most famous poet, and certainly her word choice and general meter suited us on the whole. We spent many hours that night, after hearing the news, discussing over drinks who might next succeed her as our most famous poet, but it was soon apparent that it may be some time before we can say for certain that there is another famous poet from our country.

17

An Allentown man turned on his mother, he would later tell the court, for having set a *poor example.*

18

A Calgary woman sued her Internet service provider for psychological damages from what she called leaky WiFi, believing rogue fields to be causing her headaches and palpitations, and citing as evidence numerous anecdotal accounts of having felt better during interruptions of service. The judge, having failed to reason with the woman as to the likely sources of her anxiety, negotiated a waving of the Internet service provider's usual disconnection fees, a settlement which she declined, saying that she would very much like to keep her access, but would simply prefer that it did not leak.

19

After damning implements were seized, a readymade artist had been found guilty of fabrication.

20

A Pennsylvania judge did not accept the testimony of a young artist who had claimed, as a defense of his recent spate of suicide attempts, that he lacked an audience for his work, specific to rare modes of the human condition as it was. The artist was sentenced to a psychiatric rehabilitation center and, subsequently, a marketing course at the local community college, for which the state would pay a portion.

21

A prominent writer of online hotel reviews who popularized the notion that, just as the gallery can elevate an object to the level of art by removing it from all context and forcing us to contemplate the *thing itself,* the hotel elevates human life in much the same way, died at home in his bed.

22

A male writer of an older generation, seeing what he had done, engaged Control+F in order to quickly remedy the imbalance of passive pronouns.

23

It had occurred to one writer of prose, only after his third divorce, that he had been writing poor female characters for a number of years.

24

A friend with whom I had been dining at a famous hotel just off Times Square expressed suddenly, just after salad, that he had succeeded in automating much of his job by way of simple scripts and suggestion algorithms, leaving him in a moral quandary over whether or not to inform his managers of the futility of his continued employment, accepting the risk for the potential return of a promotion for brazen ingenuity. I suggested, in jest, that before going to his superiors he should write a similar script to automate managerial procedure in order to make a careful point. He had already done this, he informed me, and had lost his job in every simulation to date.

25

The atomic bomb, it was argued by a noted philosopher, had managed to undermine the human capacity for sincerity by rendering all ideologies suspect in response to the sudden implosion of scientific progress as a quasi-religious ideal. The shell of linguistic irony that exists today, ushered in by the postmodernists, could be traced to that very event, he argued, in essence the *first modern knock-knock joke*. It was this final remark that warranted discipline.

26

There had been, a generation ago, a formal proposal by the Nevada Board of Tourism to the AEC requesting to build, at no expense to the federal government, a platform for the viewing of tests of the atomic bomb from a distance of only ten miles, to be set on state land and ringed by a large slab of blast-proof glass that, it was thought, would dampen the effects of any latent radiation. Many visitors, they explained, already came to Las Vegas solely to watch the sky at night for signs of atomic bomb tests, and many more were likely to come if the experience was offered more directly, though, as the memo stressed, *safely*.

27

A local religious leader, we were told near Savannah, who had been described as *progressive,* had recently announced that he would stake no position on the ultimate identity of dark matter.

28

Rumors out of Texas that a technophobic cult had abducted several autistic savants in order to use them as biological computers had prompted a raid, which found only registered firearms.

29

In November of last year, an IT manager in Tustin was fired after installing on every machine in his office a program that would display an occasional reminder that the company had the explicit right to review thorough logs of user activity on any computer that it owned, including browser history. While the practice was well within company policy, and at least two employees had been terminated due to licentious use of company property in the past, the notifications, the company felt, had created a threatening work environment.

30

A sleep psychologist at Princeton who had, for a number of years, done top-notch research on the effects of various types of fatty acids on the somnolent brain and won many grants for her brilliant work, was awarded a rather prestigious grant that has traditionally been somewhat of a lifetime achievement award, given to researchers toward the end of their careers so that they might pursue long-neglected pet projects. Upon receiving the grant, she promptly announced that she would be suspending her current study on the effects of avocado oil on the ultradian sleep cycle in favor of an extensive survey designed to determine the identities of background actors in dreams. She reported that no serious research had been done into the matter, and she was eager to learn whether they represented visual noise, innate character archetypes, or dormant images of past acquaintances no longer accessible through conscious recall. There was, she announced, also the possibility that they were ghosts. Ignoring questions on the latter point, she was asked by a reporter from the Herald just how she planned to go about getting information about, by definition, the least likely part of one's dream to be remembered. *I suppose I will just have to ask them,* meaning the subjects, *to pay better attention.*

31

In a national survey, it was determined that more Americans could define the word *transcendental* than could name more than half of the current Supreme Court justices. No wonder, wrote one pundit, as the most common classroom dictionary defines transcendental as *having the quality of transcendence,* whereas the names of the current Supreme Court justices are not even listed.

32

One wonders not only what effect the ability to ask questions of elaborately connected databases will have on the sorts of perspectives we take on human life, but also what interstices may be discovered in which the inner workings of human experience will remain hopelessly opaque: for instance, that three people in the last century share the official cause of death, *drowned in a rainstorm.*

33

In the spring, an Arizona man accused of drunkenly swerving his car onto a busy sidewalk, killing just one man while injuring a dozen other passersby, became the first person I am aware of to have used a variant of multiverse theory as a criminal defense. The man stated before the judge that, because every *decision* effectively splits the universe in two, with both possibilities existing simultaneously in every such case, there was no avoiding the existence of a universe in which he had not decided to drive home that evening and in which the deceased was sound and intact, barring circumstances unrelated to himself. He had no doubt, he told the judge, when prodded further about why then, if that was the case, that the judge should not pronounce him guilty now, as there was also then a universe in which he would be innocent, that there were surely more universes than not in which he had acted cogently and responsibly. There, it was decided, his argument lacked elegance.

34

In Porto Alegre, we met an engineer who claimed to still have code lingering in the latest version of an enterprise software system first constructed — though since updated almost beyond recognition — over two decades ago. He was brought to our hotel bar by a younger woman, a local, whom we looked upon with amusement and suspicion, as he went on to tell us, in no uncertain terms, that you should never do work for anyone without first negotiating a stake in the outcome, stock options at a reasonable strike price being most preferable. It had been, after several drinks, impossible for us to ascertain whether his tone implied that he had or had not received just compensation for his role in the enterprise software, but his companion, perhaps demonstrating a knack for that sort of thing, had by then disappeared, and we found ourselves helping him back to his hotel some miles away.

35

There had been another bar that evening at which I met a man who, when I remarked that he seemed rather unsteady on his bar stool and perhaps would rather join me at a low table, confided in me that he suffered from a rare but in-fact-verified condition, a strain of vertigo that was due to the very rotation of the earth, a momentum that, he assured me, could be felt by a select few, among whom fewer still were actually made ill by the acute awareness of the distance above the earth's core, spinning faster as it does, at which they sit, a malady termed Chandler's Vertigo. Though fascinated, I had to excuse myself, having no head for post-Copernican anxieties.

36

According to a popular search engine, the rate of incidence of the phrase *Theseus's Paradox* in text documents has coincided roughly with rate of organ transplants over the course of the last hundred years, though often without the post-apostrophal *s*.

37

A respected author, whom we all admired and who had written many a sentence to be jealous of, was forced to leave a workshop at a liberal arts college in Maine for failing to defend her most recent book to a student in light of postcolonialism; the jeers, she said, she could still hear in her head some weeks later.

38

A debate between linguists, on whether the shape of human thought more closely resembled poetry or more closely resembled prose, had come to blows.

39

A Houston man awoke from an operation to find he was some-one other than he had been before, causing a minor scandal. The hospital released a press statement saying that this was a rare, though documented, side effect of a certain anesthetic, the primary active ingredient of which, in its unprocessed form, is used in certain spiritual exercises in deeper Paraguay. For prac-tical reasons, the hospital declined to comment on the nature of the operation, citing the privacies of the patient. A common error of agreement.

40

It is a fair question, whether or not the difference between hoarding and collecting isn't simply a matter of square footage. The smell of a dead cat, crushed to death under a stack of fallen newspapers, brought the authorities to the apartment of a friend's aunt. Several of us later accompanied our friend to provide moral support as she tried to convince her aunt of the litany of symptoms she was presenting, certain disorders of the personality being near impossible to rule out. Her aunt would only reply that she didn't *want to be on television,* and we all left, discouraged.

41

Faced with a lack of contingent examples on which to base official policy, the director of a government agency had commissioned a program in which writers of speculative fiction were asked to imagine alternatives to the modern Internet, particularly among more primitive peoples. One of the responses, which proved nauseating to the director of the agency, mentioned the possibility of a discreet network made from the *stitched-together nervous systems of insects.*

42

It was at a retrospective for an artist once called *terminally figurative,* but whom we were now celebrating, I met a rather terse man who had, after having his curiosity boil over, asked to see my phone for a few moments. When he handed it back to me, he remarked that he was immensely impressed with the weather.

43

A petition, with the near-unanimous support of the residents of a North Carolina town of fewer than five hundred residents, was sent to the developers of a popular weather app, requesting that it recognize their township instead of defaulting their weather to that of a neighboring city of a *more respectable census.*

44

One of the primary features of late capitalism, we are told, is that corporate entities will seek to become entrenched as infrastructure, a survival strategy against whatever reckoning is to come. A San Mateo man, owing to this very feature, recently admitted to having included in the source code of a traffic control system, which has been operating in several major West Coast cities since the early nineties, a script that would cause an overnight caution light near SFO to blink, in Morse code, his name, social security number, and other bits of identifying information exactly once per lunar cycle. The confession came after it was announced that, due to the system's reliance on a single server running Windows '95, the software would be replaced entirely within two years. He had, he would later say, not foreseen the obsolescence of Morse code.

45

A local man, believed by most to be something of a good Samaritan, had taken to throwing bricks through the windshields of cars whose alarms had gone off extendedly and during odd hours of the night. Police would later determine, however, that the brick often preceded the alarm, and that the man, who had been considered psychologically unwell, was in the wrong regardless of the order of events.

46

Though the peculiar effects of great wealth on individuals have been thoroughly documented, new variants are quick to appear. A film producer, who earned his hundred-odd credits mostly through cash contributions rather than creative insight, would often insist on having production meetings at his home outside of Costa Mesa, where he kept several large bags of heroin, arranged haphazardly on his kitchen counter, by which guests would invariably have to file, a jarring sight given his reputation as a man who didn't so much as trust a strong tea. Friends and clients would, posthumously, accuse him of using the heroin, which was determined to be authentic during an estate inventory, as a method of intimidation, and indeed no one in the decade of this practice so much as mentioned it to an outside party. The heroin has now been cemented in posterity as a mark of his eccentricity, which, this reminds us, is something afforded only to the very rich or the very poor.

47

The phrase *a wheelbarrow of bricks* appears in a disproportionate number of polemics critical of radical feminism, reports a journal thought to be unbiased.

48

Patterns of language, we are told, frequently disseminate memetically without ever having to be codified, such that many traffic accidents nationwide are officially reported as having been the fault of an *unspecific dog.*

49

A persistent bit of advice to venture capitalists is never to trust a *novel verb.*

50

The murder of a wife and her two children by a jealous ex-lover had been called, perhaps to differentiate the headline from all the others, *gratuitous.*

51

My great uncle had been the architect of a great barn-inspired structure in upstate New York, said to be in the Czech style, that had been used as the painting space of a well-known abstract expressionist, who only requested of the building that it be *serviceable*. It had been, for a while, a popular tourist destination, before reviews appeared online warning potential visitors that, while there is no doubt an *aura* about the place, there is not a single trace of the artist to be found, and certainly none of the mad dashes of color he had been known for, which one might reasonably have expected to carelessly adorn a wall or beam. It was only after my great uncle's diary was uncovered, it being of some import due to the magnitude of some of his clients and his meticulous note-taking about specific requests, that it was learned that the interior walls of the barn had been white when the building was completed, per the artist's request, and that the wood grain, thought to bear no sign of the artist's hand had, in fact, been entirely painted on, over a plain white canvas. The tourism business has once again picked up, but they have had to install a rope so that visitors do not get too close.

52

A well-collected painter of our town had lost the use of his right hand in an accident and promptly retired from painting. We would often ask him, in one way or another, why he could not simply learn to paint with the left hand, to which he invariably answered *balance*. And when we would devise, on the spot, methods by which he could steady himself at the easel — for he was known for his large, violent brushstrokes — he would tell us, invariably, that we had not understood. His auction prices have not yet steadied after the accident, with one critic noting that it was hard to determine whether or not he should, for market purposes, *be considered dead.*

53

A University of Chicago study revealed that among individuals who have sought psychiatric counseling for so-called impostor syndrome, that is, a belief that one is under- or unqualified to do the work one has been assigned, more than eighty percent had job titles that did not appear on a census form before 1990.

54

A man went to the doctor complaining that he could not sleep at night, troubled as he was by the CIA's deposing of a democratically elected leader in Guatemala in 1954, not least because the United Fruit Corporation had played such an invidious role in order to continue their unfair labor practices. The doctor, after jotting down some notes, said he would not prescribe the man anything, and that it was simply best not to *think about such things.*

55

An autodidact who had learned a great deal, perhaps even all there is to know, about contemporary philosophy by watching lectures from all of the great teachers of the day online, marched into the office of the head of the philosophy department at a prominent university and demanded a faculty position, and then proceeded to rattle off an impeccably constructed argument that adroitly melded two previously discontinuous strains of continental thought as a demonstration of his mastery of the subject matter. Before the department head had been able to respond, the autodidact turned and walked away, having realized something of the nature of the academy.

56

A philosopher giving a lecture highlighting the nuances of Hegel's concept of *abstract universality* said that the Internet had made it possible for all of us to live quite intimately with the concept on a daily basis, and asked rhetorically if the students had ever *really* grasped what the Internet *is* in itself, instead of defining it negatively against all else. One student, capable in such matters, explained.

57

It is a law of history, some may have you believe, that one cannot be at the height of their powers for more than a generation. A great philosopher of the postmodern and intellectual hero of mine, I learned while sitting in his office, cannot properly format a hyperlink.

58

A formal apology was issued by an academic to the people of Tuvalu, for likening *working in serious semiotics to living on an island slowly sinking into the ocean.* A follow-up trip is planned.

59

Murder, a once-popular crime novelist lamented, used to be *more interesting.*

60

It was once cautioned by a popular daytime television host to never combine a social media account with that of a significant other, as it had been shown by psychologists to cause difficult-to-reverse trauma at the end of a relationship. *Even if they threaten suicide.*

61

In one hundred years, we will speak almost entirely in verbs. Yale.

62

It has been noted that, for a confluence of reasons, the average age for authors of debut novels has dropped dramatically over the last twenty years, and continues to drop steadily, though at a slower pace than it has dropped for much of the last twenty years. While it is commonly accepted that the rise of MFA programs is largely the cause, it may also be that prodigiousness, the requirements for which once extended well into one's twenties, now stops at around fourteen, art being more like tennis.

63

The concept of the Anthropocene was proposed originally — by another name — by a Roman, who believed that such a signifi-cant portion of the rocks on Earth had been moved or otherwise shaped by human hands that it marked an entirely new era in history, even though his estimate was still quite conservative.

64

A woman, 64, of Ohio who had, her entire life, wished to be remarkable enough to appear in the local paper, a dream owing to a small feature done on her father the unionist, which had been framed and hung in her home as a child, committed suicide upon hearing the paper was to be discontinued, a skeleton crew to staff a small corner of the web to keep the silence at bay. She was able to make the obituaries.

65

A woman of Tallahassee filed an official appeal to the state to allow her to marry a rubberized implement, citing its egoless qualities.

66

Outside of Spokane, a man and a woman quarreled over the former's fanatic interest in professional wrestling, which he agreed was *indeed* not a sport, but insisted, per Roland Barthes, possessed qualities that put it in the same category as Greek tragedy, namely the omnipresent struggle of good versus evil with few shades of grey, the stage allowing little nuance, after which she allegedly took a hatchet to him.

67

A cesspool of our attentive imaginations, wrote an advertising executive. Budgetary considerations.

68

A presiding senator who had spent his past two terms as part of the education committee, first as a member and later as chairman, and who was later implicated in attempting to solicit sexual favors from his male interns, said on camera that feminist critiques of the core curriculum, especially in the area of US history, were *disgusting*. It is wrong, I find, for the media to insist on identifying the gender of the interns, if we are to make progress at all in some areas.

69

There is a roving band of miscreants whose sole occupation is to harass and intimidate grade-school teachers of United States history, namely those who *insist* that the French had a hand in England's defeat during the Revolution. It is a process that one member, when cornered for an interview, termed *exhaustive,* though it seems likely he misspoke.

70

There is a dark strain of political humor in which holding a loaded gun to your head in order to have your demands acquiesced to is known as a *Cheyenne filibuster.*

71

When asked, during a talk on either content as form or form as content, how architects could justify their practices in light of the fact that much of their time was spent lobbying wealthy patrons for private commissions that could not, by definition, bring about the sort of radical changes in context by way of spatial reconsideration being discussed, a prominent draftsman responded that he had no defense prepared and, smiling, encouraged the inquisitive student to perhaps lead his own revolution someday, before ducking the stucco brick that had been hurled at his head.

72

We are told now that our brains are constantly simulating the future, using the sensory data of one moment like a film still to predict the next. It was after developing the belief that he had become acutely aware of this process that a clinical psychologist found himself in regular care, being bathed by nurses and all else that is entailed. He lamented that he could not in any way take advantage of his ability, and further, that it was, as one might expect, really quite annoying.

73

A man whom we engaged in conversation in a bar in Cincinnati, we learned, was what he himself had termed a *freelance lobbyist,* who spoke to local governments out of concern for a little-known practice of the electronics industry, who had colluded, in earlier years, to calibrate all of their digital clocks with slight discrepancies, such that steady time was never kept, seconds were compressed and dilated, added and subtracted as needed, resulting in a persistent, barely perceptible disorientation, a phenomenon he himself had termed AMTD, or Artificial Micro-Time Dilations. A secondary concern had been that the sudden corrections may cause real-time experiences to compress like memories, rendering much of life indistinguishable from memory; but, he said, this was more difficult to prove.

74

After some admitted extravagances, a proposed bill to cap government spending on governmental buildings was settled, declaring as reasonable a mere $250,000 per Congressional head, just as a group of Senators had been accused of gerrymandering.

75

A professor of anthropology at a Northwest institution, who had until recent been most famous for his cultural studies of niche pornography and, in particular, the monograph *Lesbian Cowgirls of Budapest,* was dismissed for violating a university conduct statute, which requires no further detail.

76

After arguing that presentation should in no way be tied to the value of her art, which could loosely be considered conceptual on the grounds that it often presented difficulty with regard to exhibition, Lucia Khudobina was awarded an open-ended grant, to be continued so long as she would remain in an isolated cabin and produce nothing but the ethereal ideas that were not merely the *basis* for her art, quoting her, but the *entirety of* her art, eschewing all transferable means of representation. She was careful to make clear, after declining the grant, that she had meant what she said, but found it distasteful that the grant had been traditionally awarded for *performance art.*

77

The rich of certain enclaves, it is said, have all outfitted their homes with tanks that submerge them in saline for long enough to silence the bleating of their prefrontal cortices.

78

Comedy's existence being itself play on the void, one stand-up prefers the first row of seats at every show to be empty. In small rooms, a single empty table.

79

I have learned recently, through no fault of my own, that several companies that offer cryogenic freezing have augmented their services to include, at a slight additional cost, the careful preservation of your electronic devices, so long as a commercial charging mechanism is *reasonably available.* A USB drive can often be stored for no additional cost.

80

I had taken an uncle to a psychologist once over his insistence that Richard Dawson had never appeared on *Hogan's Heroes,* episodes of which, still in syndication, we would watch together on Wednesday evenings, and without fail I would point out that Richard Dawson was right there on screen, playing Corporal Newkirk, after which he would offer some new theory on either how the film had been doctored long after the original series had aired, or how the man wasn't even Richard Dawson to begin with, alternating theories every other week. The psychologist told me, after I had admitted that this was perhaps my uncle's only eccentricity and that he had never shown any signs of being a danger to himself or others, that his services were not necessary, and that I should be happy with my uncle's health, even in spite of his comparatively *minor divergence from reality.*

81

One artist, known as a provocateur, caused a stir when speaking at a museum event when he commented on sculpture's *leering and lurid dimensionality,* saying that too much of it relied on sexual overtones from which the viewer couldn't distance themselves in the way they could in a painting, summing up his thesis by saying that the public *won't appreciate it as art if they can fuck it.*

82

A man who leapt from a twelve-story building had thought himself a bureaucrat.

83

In a recent national poll, forty-seven percent of Americans would rather be *wrong for the right reasons,* as opposed to forty-nine who would rather be *right for the wrong reasons*; only four percent had asked for further context.

84

An art historian, author of the critical work *Degrees of Derivation,* argued publicly that the last great, original painter was Hogarth.

85

It had been irreparably damaging, because of the aptness of the metaphor, for a new branch of psychoanalysis, announced in a prominent journal as incorporating deconstructivist theory in an attempt to relieve patients of destructive metaphors, to be called *little more than* CBT *with similes.*

86

A real estate agent we met at a bar in Southern California once told us that, not only do nearly half of all of the multi-million-dollar custom homes commissioned by celebrities never resell, some have come into total disrepair and have since been claimed by uniquely segmented ecosystems. An atrium in the home of one movie star of the sixties is now the sole breeding ground of a new species of moth, which has yet to breed successfully outside of the home, the tone of his voice suggesting some hidden irony.

87

A businessman, the son of the founder of a great many appliance stores throughout the Midwest, had purchased a burial plot atop a hill in what is considered the most desirable of *resting communities* (the exact phrase from the brochure). Upon the early stages of preparation, which consisted of a pre-excavation to make the eventual, live burial rock- and root-free, a shabby coffin containing the remains of a woman and an infant, very likely buried without sanction around the turn of the century, was uncovered. The businessman, acting in what he believed to be the only fair manner, agreed charitably to cover the cost of their cremation, and the spreading of their ashes *somewhere nice.*

88

Existentialism is for the unmarried. Graffiti.

89

Until recently, there had been a man living in the Lower East Side of Manhattan, in what is called now NoLiTa by real estate agents and those who have lived in the city for less than a decade, who refused to give up a rent-controlled apartment for which he paid three-hundred twenty dollars a month, but for which a new management company believed they could get as much as ten times. He had refused to speak with them for some months, knowing that they represented Chinese interests rather than Italian, but eventually the lump sum offer grew so great as to dissuade the man from staying, the money being plenty enough to retire to Tyrol near distant family, which had likely been his final thought before collapsing on the floor, dead, just before signing the papers. His son, who lived with him, but who had not been present for the negotiations, having now inherited the lease under a succession clause, was frightened into taking three months' rent at the present rate, believing the alternative to be certain eviction and the sort of shame that would have surely killed his father.

90

The official recommendation of the American Institute for Interrelational Psychology is to restrict your number of friends on a given network to within ten percent of Dunbar's Number, saying severe departures represent potential warning signs that can and should be referenced in the DSM-4.

91

There is a well-sourced rumor that there is still such a thing as the House Assassinations Committee, and that they meet for lunch on Thursdays. There is also a competing theory that a group of Representatives who meet for lunch on Thursdays has been nicknamed the *House Assassinations Committee.*

92

Among participants in a study who preferred to indicate laughter phonetically rather than acronymically, eighty percent were found to have a negative view of the future of language.

93

A virus that has reappeared in certain parts of the country for the first time in half a century is said to be no threat to *responsible individuals,* one health official was quoted as saying. So far, eighteen have died.

94

At a bar in Oregon we met a woman who, in spite of never having so much as left her home state, was able to give expert recommendations and assessments of restaurants in any US city, surprising us in many cases with her knowledge of hole-in-the-wall eateries and ill-publicized neighborhood favorites, solely based on her hobby of reading restaurant reviews online, both professional and amateur. She said that there was always a way to cut through critical language and find a bit of truth in any review, positive or negative, and that she hoped to work her way through Canada in the next several months.

95

A man who had been sitting next to us in a bar for some hours all at once confided in us that his father, now deceased, would buy, after every election, a bumper sticker featuring the names of the winning candidates, and he had never asked his father whether or not this was a display of bipartisan solidarity, or simply wishing to appear part of the winning team. He had also, he continued, been drinking soda the entire time.

96

A full day of a recent linguistics conference was spent debating whether or not there could, in a purely semantic sense, be such a thing as a *literal interpretation.*

97

An aging writer who had achieved fame at a relatively young age and, over the years, maintained a level of quality and acclaim sufficient for an archive to exist, in a university library basement, of his various drafts and effects, including the crumpled remains of an unfinished first novel, which would remain as such until the technology came along to allow proper uncrumpling of decades-old paper without risking the integrity of the words. Later in life, he would often pause over the trashcan, wondering aloud whether a page or a banana peel were *fit for the archive.* It is said that this was a kind of mania.

98

A mathematician, speaking at a well-attended conference on string theory and certain advanced forms of math, had used the opportunity to instead suggest a new paradigm: everything that can be proved true in math, he suggested, in order to be true must describe some feature of the existing universe, citing the most recent example of an obscure branch of research into Mersenne primes that corresponds nicely to the certain topological features of heterotic string theory. Surely, someone countered, this is not the first time that it has been noticed that one abstraction resembled another, and charged him with Platonism for the sake of Platonism.

99

It is disheartening for many so-called techno-utopianists that the most popular searches in many authoritarian countries, for which the Internet could represent a liberating social infrastructure, are still pornographic in nature.

100

It is disappointing, wrote one fellow at a prominent institute for genetic research, that the public discourse over the development of artificial lifeforms has been tainted by *the same old moral arguments.*

101

Without even realizing, a student who had travelled to Hunter College from far uptown, where rents remained feasible, and who had been evidently hardened by some months in the city, had thrust his shoulder into that of a man who had been standing directly in front of the nascent doors on the platform, and had walked on without consideration, making it to 60th Street before thinking about the possibility that the gentleman had been mentally ill, or blind, or perhaps both; nor had it occurred to him to remove his earbuds to hear if the man had asked forgiveness for the inconvenience. The student, late already to a seminar on comparative literature or some such, determined to continue, and only later throw himself in front of the next available express train.

102

Humanity has been a great putting on and taking off of opinions.
A bumper sticker.

103

A magnate left, as the only written account of his life, a note to his son advising that he should never leave a massage *before you feel like you've had the shit kicked out of you.* This, now widely quoted.

104

Only this year, an association of optometrists officially recognized a condition known as *Velma Syndrome,* applied to those who, for fear of waking up in the midst of a traumatic situation and not being able to find their glasses, sleep in their contact lenses to the point of causing corneal ulcers. This does not account for those who hold the same fear in spite of perfect vision.

105

An oil worker from Nome, 56, shot himself in the head after his search for *younger women* returned an error. The man, who had been encouraged by his grown children to use the Internet to meet women some years after his wife had died in a tragic car accident, and who had never possessed the time nor compunction to become computer literate, had believed the error to have almost certainly flagged him as a pedophile. A server had been temporarily unreachable.

106

There had been a temporary ban on Camus in university book-stores after a report surfaced in a distinguished, if declining, magazine that estimated that the French-Algerian's work could be found in better than a third of the dorm rooms of college students who commit suicide within their first year away from home, more than six times the rate of the next author on the list. The dean of a small Wesleyan college said that he had made the decision after a nationwide string of lawsuits aimed at institutions for not doing more to protect students. He had to do *something*.

107

Some seventeen Beckett scholars have disappeared or retreated from public life under mysterious circumstances over the course of the past four decades, as reported by an expert on such matters.

108

The philosopher Neary had, after nearly a decade of research, compiled what was widely hailed as the most incredible compendium of critical opinions on the deserved academic fate of so-called Nazi intellectuals, as given by other Western intellectuals over the last forty-odd years. He was asked, during an interview preceding publication of the book — titled *Critical Opinions on Gifted Nazis: A Compendium,* appropriately — why he had undertaken that particular project, and responded, *Because the facts show no mercy.* He was widely misquoted.

109

A man who quit his job in Tucson in order to complete a screen-play, the title of which he had possessed in one form or another since he was a young boy even though the content had changed drastically, had re-applied for his old position after learning that there had already been a film of the same title made, well before he was born. His script was, by all accounts, remarkably original, but he could not bring himself to call it by another name.

110

A respected medical journal was forced to print an apology for the contents of a recent paper by a reproductive endocrinologist on the relationship between postpartum depression and the use of epidurals in which the author, seeking to link the pain of childbirth to the strength of motherly instincts, had called the bond between mother and child *a flavor of Stockholm syndrome.*

111

A tourist, who had spent more than a week visiting San Antonio, El Paso, and Austin, and who by any measure had seen the pertinent cultural and historical sites both in and between the cities, had killed a man at a truck stop west of Abilene, having decided, he told the jury, that Texas wasn't all it was cracked up to be.

112

A Barstow man accused of the second degree murder of his longtime girlfriend over her passing resemblance to an Internet porn model, whose picture had been sent to him by his best friend, whom in reality he only merely tolerated. He was reportedly *devastated* to learn that the passing resemblance had been just that, and that the model in question had been from Belgrade. Still, the opinion of his best friend had to count for something.

113

A well-known eccentric some years ago had said that hope for mankind was lost as soon as it built a machine it could not lift.

114

A young boy had been shot, separate from the one the day before.

115

The notion that a person dies a sort of genuine death when their name is spoken for the last time, having become increasingly popular with secularists in recent years, has led to the founding of a not-for-profit organization that assures users that after death, in exchange for regular dues paid while alive, two or more volunteers will have a conversation about you on your birthday (or a given day of your choice) based on available photos and information, much of which is submitted via an online questionnaire. It is required of the volunteers, according to the terms and conditions, to *wonder what you were like*.

116

The fact that so many had failed foresee the advent of replacement organs grown from stem cells proved that there had been a decided lack of imagination on the part of this most recent crop of science-fiction authors, wrote one commentator on the short-lived phenomenon of clone literature.

117

A university professor had been fired for using the word *mixed* to refer to a hypothetical subset of students who had parents of different racial backgrounds, being first scolded by the head of the department of humanities for violating the department's official policy on race's status as a social construct, and then given condolences by the dean, who told him the board had been forced by donors, sensitive to the issues of today, to take action on the next disciplinary case which could be said to be at all *racial*.

118

A history professor was severely reprimanded by the board of the university for using the pronoun *we* when describing the accomplishments of early Polynesian shipbuilders, he himself being from Augsburg. History, as it is taught, he explained, promotes a false sense of tribal competition, such that students take away the implicit notion that, living in a modern, developed nation, they have somehow won, and others lost. This was not, as decided by a vote, a noble enough justification.

119

A popular philosopher in the psychoanalytic tradition with a bent toward Hegel, having agreed to take part in a Q&A session on the website of a London newspaper, was asked by a student from Lucerne just how much longer, given the nature of enterprise, the rapid progress in machine learning, and the approaching epistemic break at which the advance of technology will outpace communication thereof, even as communication has nearly become predictive, that it was practical to be a philosopher in the psychoanalytic tradition with a bent toward Hegel? Lacan, he answered, would have a field day with all of the new specimens of Otherness brought on by these new forms of technology, but Hegel, he continued, would probably struggle with texting. This, a joke.

120

The family of a hiker who had been trekking across the Scottish countryside was notified of his almost certain death by way of an automated email alert tied to an application which required the user to check in once a week at a predetermined time or be presumed dead, their social media accounts closed, pertinent passwords divulged to next of kin, and their family and friends notified in one of five ways, based on user preference, email being the most common. The fact that his death had been reported a day early was assumed by his family, in their state of grief, to have been due to the difference in time zones.

121

It is a positive sign for equality, wrote one sociologist, that fewer married men who commit suicide feel it necessary to kill their wives as well, believing them capable.

122

Papers detailing genetic differences between waves of early human migration in terms of the added genetic materials of other
hominids should be disseminated carefully, given the *intellectual bent* of some twenty-first-century racism. A paper from a
Midwestern school.

123

There had not been sufficient warnings, we have now been told, and the safety guidelines are to be revisited. Nine children.

124

A teacher has come under fire in the town of Humboldt for warning her children that, when working in groups, the tendency to allow one student to do the bulk of the work because they are more *capable* is tantamount to fascism.

125

Daniels, of Newark, had thrown an axe through a conference room window after being dismissed for having been unwilling to answer an email over the weekend. The presence of the axe, though, indicates a conflicting prescience.

126

Five harbor seals, pressured by warmer waters to seek food else-where, crossed a busy street near Cambria, watched intently by idling motorists.

127

It is true, it was conceded by a critic, that we are given more opportunities, today, to grow as adults to love the childish things that we did not have the chance to love as children.

128

The certitude of relativists is the most repugnant. A bumper sticker.

129

Near one of the great cities of the Pacific Northwest, four armed men were arrested after having stopped several brigades of passing motorists and asked the passengers, with pointed tones, for paperwork that would firmly establish citizenship, their stated motive being to slow or altogether halt globalization.

130

Division in the Flat-Earth Community. A headline.

131

A Massachusetts town has been implicated in a decades-old crime after it was discovered during the replacement of a rotting section of telephone line that much of the cable present had in fact belonged to a neighboring city and had been reported stolen in 1936. The fence, only twelve at the time of the crime, confessed.

132

Some ten years ago, several video game bloggers reported to the FBI that they had been mistakenly contacted by men claiming to be FSB officers, who believed them to be dissidents of a potentially violent nature, based on transcriptions by a rudimentary translation software. Ten men came forward; an eleventh was later arrested on weapons charges, leaving a ratio that was called *terribly misleading* by the authorities.

133

A councilman, who had served less than an entire term in his political career, cautioned against the imposition of an added tax on food and beverages sold at venues that are supported by taxpayer money, saying the city would face a revolt if the plan so much as became public. He was duly reminded of the year, evidently to imply that the people had not revolted for some time.

134

A man whom we encountered in yet another pub, who had been quite drunk and nonchalantly threatening to take his own life, admitted after we offered him a glass of water that he was doing little more than acting out every cliché of depression that he had ever read about or seen, in what he had termed, after Baudrillard, *representations of life from which it is impossible to hide,* and in truth had no idea how he should channel his grief at the world in a more genuine fashion. We suggested that perhaps that depiction was so prevalent because it could not help but exist, in light of the fact that it was the most genuine available representation of acedia, after which we conceded that while there had been some promise shown in cognitive behavioral therapy, we all preferred the alcohol.

135

After a judge declared in a case of mutual assault between two men of differing faiths that religion had *never entered into it,* he attended to the matter of one man's broken jaw.

136

On the grounds of performance art, a man charged one of the stainless steel balloon dogs on display and began stabbing at it with a kitchen knife, shouting *sic semper tyrannis.* The clanging, as described by an onlooker, was incessant.

137

Certain statistical institutions still insist on categorizing the cause of some suicides as melancholy, even though there have been no official diagnoses in some decades. Also, there are grumblings that what we call the nightingale is, in reality, two separate species.

138

A work of immersive theater, titled *Set a Small Fire for a Soldier,* had been forced to close after only two performances. In the first act, a dying man, dressed in desert fatigues and clearly sporting a gunshot wound, crawls into an expansive space, into which the audience has already been ushered, and begs their help to build a fire, lest he die then and there. It was to be assumed that, once a fire had been made, he would tell them his story, and other characters would follow, complicating matters. In both performances, the audience remained still for so long that, according to the actor, he had *no choice but to die.*

139

A Billings man, who had resigned himself to his basement with its stores of ammo and canned goods, some years ago, recently put the main floor of his home up for rent, citing separate means of egress.

140

A judge had no answer for a woman who asked why her husband, who had tried to murder her in cold blood but had failed, owing to a complete lack of familiarity with firearms, had received a lesser sentence than that which was typically handed down for murder for no other reason than his own incompetence.

141

An ambient musician who claimed to have tape loops perform-
ing in every governmental office in Ohio was found to be a fraud
after bomb squads found nothing. Reported in the *Times*.

142

Several of us, who had not seen each other in many years, fell easily into the same old arguments, only now better informed in the same positions. One-by-one, one of us would shake the hands of all the others before excusing themselves to some duty or another, until the two of us remaining had little left to do but agree.

143

An artist, whose latest exhibition involved sitting on a stool with a knife held against his left ankle with his right hand, began, in the face of a bemused patron, sawing at his tendons. The patron clapped.

144

Those who are rich are often rich in many ways. When a house-keeper, whose sole occupation was to dwell in the guest home of a wealthy couple in order to maintain its *lived-in* qualities, committed suicide in that very home last May, her employers ventured that it may have been the bite of a particular kind of bug that drove her to it, citing a local doctor, an osteopath.

145

There are promises that, with improvements to fMRI technology, what *matters* to us will become more clear.

146

A unique feature of religion being that nearly every atheist who began life in a religious household is said to have an answer prepared, should the unlikely happen. A study out of Washington.

147

It has been discussed at a high level whether or not to regulate the use of serifs in fine print, though only as a matter of accessibility.

148

A nationwide survey conducted by an institute for philosophical research has determined that nihilists, on the whole, have good intentions.

149

Two philosophers, who had been arguing for some decades over whether *irony* or *absurdity* was the essence of this late stage in history, and who had fallen out — sometimes to the point of routine violence — on more than one occasion over the years, had reconciled once again in order to participate in their first debate since the widespread adoption of the Internet. The philosopher who favored irony as the prime condition of modern humors began with a victory statement, as he believed that irony had become the *de facto* language of the Internet, every statement carrying a duplicitous meaning indicative of an understanding of the cultural circumstances which breed such conditions as this, irony being the by-product of the continual reconciliation of contradictions, an awareness of our *piteous contingency,* now more or less a natural state. The second philosopher countered that this exercise was a half-hearted one at best, a Sisyphean task that has engendered a hopelessness that has allowed for the complete divorce of meaning from content, a divorce marred by *irreconcilable differences.* The two philosophers, in the end, agreed to no future debates after the school paper had chosen to run with the headline: **;) vs. :P**

150

It is quietly festering, said one neurologist, the knowledge that we can be controlled by more than our own will, and that a will may well be a series of unconnected impulses selected for by our many underlying modes of generating internal narrative to fit the unconscious circuitry that has, by and large, already decided for us. It was, on the whole, a stupid speech.

For more information:

joshuarothes.com
@joshuarothes
istheauthordead.com
isthenoveldead.com

"W. dreams, like Phaedrus, of an army of thinker-friends, thinker-lovers. He dreams of a thought-army, a thought-pack, which would storm the philosophical Houses of Parliament. He dreams of Tartars from the philosophical steppes, of thought-barbarians, thought-outsiders. What distance would shine in their eyes!"

— Lars Iyer

Made in the USA
San Bernardino, CA
20 January 2017